gardening & planting by the mon

by the

2024

James Lynn Page

foulsham

LONDON • NEW YORK • TORONTO • SYDNEY

foulsham

An imprint of Foulsham Publishing Ltd
The Old Barrel Store, Drayman's Lane, Marlow, Bucks SL7 2FF

Foulsham books can be found in all good bookshops and direct from
www.foulsham.com

ISBN: 978-0-572-08439-6

Copyright © 2023 James Lynn Page

Cover photograph © Garden Picture Library

Series, format and layout design © 2023 Foulsham Publishing Ltd

The moral right of the author has been asserted

A CIP record for this book is available from the British Library

Typeset in India by Lapiz Digital Services, Chennai
Printed and bound in Great Britain by Short Run Press

Contents

Introduction

What, precisely, *is* lunar gardening, or agricultural astrology, or – latterly – *biodynamic* gardening? Simply put, the core idea is that cycles of the Moon affect the growth of plants. Just as we know that the Moon's gravitational pull makes the seas and oceans on the Earth's surface 'bulge' causing tides to rise and fall, the same gravitational pull affects the plants in your garden. We'll discuss this in a little more depth later, but different phases of the Moon – from one new Moon to the next – reveal different levels of activity in the natural fluids and saps contained in the leaves and roots of all plant life, as well as in the moisture in the soil. It is lunar gardening that tracks this very process and seeks to optimise the results. And that's it, in a nutshell.

The lunar gardening calendar presented in this book is a 'to-do' guide for the whole fifteen months that run from October 2023 right through to the end of 2024. Here you will find details of the best lunar gardening practices in the vegetable, fruit and flower garden, plus the traditional names of the Full Moons for each month and some old weather and agricultural lore (which some people would call superstitions). Dates and times of equinoxes and solstices are included, along with the lunar and solar eclipses, plus the times when the Moon rises and sets (often the best times of day for planting). Also, the four main 'fire festivals' from Celtic tradition are noted for the year. Look out for some of the best periods to grow medicinal or therapeutic herbs, those that are backed, to some extent, by scientific research. There is also a short glossary at the end of the book where gardening and astrology jargon is explained.

Lunar gardening has a long pedigree, yet for some it can seem to border on the superstitious. Perhaps this is because it originated at a time when the Universe was viewed in a more magical sense. Now we are better enlightened as to how it truly works, we modern astrologers even have science on our side! The old *traditional* literature on lunar gardening is pretty sparse and can be difficult to obtain. But a (relatively) new movement is afoot and interest in *modern* lunar gardening has expanded year on year since the middle of the twentieth century.

The positive results from lunar sowing and planting have been well-documented over the previous 40 or so years, and if you work with the cosmic cycles in this book, you should see a dramatic improvement in the quality of your garden produce.

So then, happy gardening!

Lunar Gardening Then and Now

For centuries people looked to the stars for omens, and planting by the phases (or quarters) of the Moon was recognised as a valid pursuit. Classical period authors including Hesiod (*fl.* 750–650 BCE), Cato the Elder (234–149 BCE), Varro (116–28 BCE) and Pliny the Elder (c. 23–79 CE) all had something to say about it. Pliny, as usual, preferred to sit on the fence and report others' findings, arguing, 'Some persons are of opinion that [the bean] should be sown at full Moon, the lentil between the twenty-fifth and thirtieth day of the Moon,... and they assure us that if this is done they will be exempt from the attacks of slugs.'[1]

And yet, in these ancient books we often see fanciful (though no doubt symbolic) rather than practical arguments. Some would say they are too superstitious. For instance, the Moon – quite apart from its physical effect on our planet – was worshipped as a manifestation of the Roman Goddess, Diana. By the seventeenth century, apparent superstitions had not abated, as when the English astrologer-botanist Nicolas Culpepper wrote about the health-giving properties of Lettuces, 'The Moon owns them, and that is the reason they cool and moisten what heat and dryness Mars causeth, because Mars has his fall in Cancer' [2]

Modern lunar gardeners have taken these cosmic principles from the ancient world and given them a new, more practical context, based on experimental data. These days, our go-to source is the Biodynamic Movement, which began with the spiritual teacher Rudolf Steiner in the early twentieth century. Steiner was the founder of Anthroposophy which, essentially, aims to unite spiritual realities with scientific/intellectual clarity. He also founded a research group, long-windedly named the Agricultural Experimental Circle of Anthroposophical Farmers and Gardeners of the General Anthroposophical Society. This group would test methods in organic farming, in particular those coming from an occult or spiritual viewpoint. Between 1924 and 1939, this group drew about 800 members from all over the world. Less than a year before his death in 1925, Steiner gave a series of lectures which are the genesis of today's lunar organic gardening. In the first lecture on 7 June 1924 in Kobierzyce, Poland, mentioning the Moon, he said that everything connected with 'the inner force of reproduction and growth and – everything that contributes to the sequence of generation after generation in the plants — works through those forces which come down from the Cosmos to the Earth.'

Steiner did, nevertheless, add that it's doubtful if we can prove such things 'by the customary physical methods of today.' But he *was* interested in what might happen if sowing and planting were carried out according to lunar phases. It was up to his followers to carry on the work, which eventually became known as Biodynamic Agriculture. Consider the next section a brief 'hall of fame' for Biodynamic Gardeners.

Soon after Steiner's death Lilly Kolisko was experimenting with metallic salts to test whether the planets had specific effects on certain metals. The salts were dissolved, and their solutions were permitted to crystallise on filter paper. Kolisko discovered an effect involving Saturn which could limit the rate of crystallization in keeping with Saturn's traditional function of 'limitation'. Later, Kolisko began a series of experiments to test the theories behind lunar gardening, discovering that plants sown before the Full Moon grew more rapidly – and satisfyingly. She reported her findings in *Moon and Plant Growth*, published in the 1930s, announcing that carrots, tomatoes, lettuce, beans, and peas flourished better and *tasted* better using lunar gardening principles. The experiments were even mentioned in the British science journal *Nature*, in 1946.

The name of Maria Thun will be well known to devotees of lunar gardening. Originally a disciple of Steiner, in the 1940s Thun attended courses at the Institute for Biodynamic Research in Darmstadt, where she encountered one Franz Rulni, who had published a planting calendar. We have Maria Thun to thank for introducing the signs of the zodiac into lunar gardening. In the 1950s she experimented with sowing radishes, discovering that they manifested in a different form and size depending on which sign the Moon occupied when they were planted.

Like the diligent researcher she was, Thun experimented further with different crops throughout the 1950s to see if lunar influence was present. She brought to the fore Plant–Element Days (a crucial feature of this book) which indicate the types of plant to work with based on the Moon's progress through the zodiac. Her legacy is the annual *Biodynamic Sowing and Planting Calendar*.

Then there is Louise Riotte – also inspired by Steiner – and who, during her lifetime, penned twelve books on biodynamic gardening, among them the highly popular *Carrots Love Tomatoes*. She had the appropriate parental background, too – she learned the art of astrology from her father whilst her mother practised herbalism. An honourable citation must also go to English master gardener and teacher Alan Chadwick, another pioneer and Steiner acolyte who became a firm advocate of organic and lunar gardening in the 60s and 70s.

Finally, we must mention the English horticulturalist and writer Charles Dowding, who touches on the subject of planting by zodiac sign on his website. Dowding writes that, 'we sowed half a bed of carrots [a Root Plant] with Moon in a water sign and half a bed one week later, when it was in a root [earth] sign. Both grew well, in fact the former looked stronger, but after weighing up the final harvest I found a 20% increase in total yield of carrots *from the root day* sowing.'[3]

Here is further evidence – if it were needed – that lunar gardening works! Yet I hasten to add, in closing, that orthodox science denies any evidence of lunar gardening, despite the admission made by *Nature* in 1946. So, what kind of evidence is there?

The 'Scientific' View

The only experimental evidence for the existence of lunar influence on the growth of land plants is that published by L. Kolisko. All other investigators in many parts of the world have been unable to discover any consistent correlation between the Moon and the vital processes of land plants; some admit that if a lunar effect does exist it is so obscure as to have no value in agricultural practice.

Nature, 1946

On the website Encyclopedia.com they comment that 'it can be argued that the Kolisko effect is as yet unverified, having as yet received little attention outside of the Anthroposophical Society, but at the same time, the amount of evidence gathered in support of it remains impressive'. What certainly isn't in doubt is the Moon's effects on everyday life in general. We've already cited its influence on the tides, but what about the Full Moon's alleged effect on humans? Isn't it supposed to make people ... shall we say, a little less restrained in their behaviour? Well, this certainly applies to the animal kingdom, and there's real documentary evidence to support that claim. Dogs, it has been found, bark more often and become agitated during a Full Moon. In a study performed at Bradford Royal Infirmary in the United Kingdom, it was found that dog bites are up to twice as frequent when the Moon is full. Vets are *definitely* aware of injuries in the dog (and cat) kingdom, which appear to increase during the Full Moon (that is, more frequently than at other times in the month). According to the LiveScience website: 'The study, reported in ... the Journal of the American Veterinary Medical Association, finds emergency room visits for these pets increases during or near the Full Moon. In studying 11,940 cases at the Colorado State University Veterinary Medical Center, the researchers found the risk of emergency room visits to be 23 per cent higher for cats and 28 per cent higher for dogs on days surrounding Full Moons ... Research into mysterious lunar connections has a long history of baffling and mixed results. A pair of studies in 2001 looked into how many humans are bitten by animals during Full Moons. British researchers found a lunar link ...'[4]

As for gardening and the Moon, an article in the *New Scientist* mentions how movements of plant leaves could be 'partially governed by the gravitational pull of the Moon', as with the tides. Noting that with some plants, their 'leaves rise and fall during the day–night cycle, as they respond to light', those that grow with an absence of light also have surprisingly 'similar cycles'. This suggests that a kind of inner regulator, like our circadian clock, may be in operation. The University of Bristol's Peter Barlow examined data on leaf movement in plants that had been recorded over the last hundred years and correlated them with computer predictions of the Moon's gravitational pull.

As *New Scientist* reported, 'The two data sets don't match exactly, says Barlow, but generally, when the lunar tide turns, so too do the leaf movements. "You've got a zero rate of change in gravity, and that seems to be the trigger for movement in the plant's cells," he says. "If you look at enough of these correlations, they all seem to be strong enough to make you believe they might be causal."'[5]

Some of the best evidence comes from Isabella Guerrini at Perugia University in Italy. The Perma-Culture Principles website draws our attention to her research which shows it's becoming more obvious that the Moon also influences water flow in plants. She writes that 'sap moves more vigorously during the waxing phase as the Moon grows to Full, and slows down as the Moon wanes to a thin morning crescent'[6] This, she explains, has important consequences for plant growth and pruning: 'vigorous, sappy plants will suffer if cut, harvested, or pruned close to the Full Moon'. She notes that 'sap from a cut plant, now deprived of its primary outlet' will even badly affect the growth of new buds, 'a phenomenon known as "lunar burn", because it was so often noted around the Full Moon'[7]

It is also important to mention the competing traditions in lunar gardening, and over at the Lunarium website they cite at least two different types – what they call the American and European versions. It hinges mainly on the kind of Zodiac one uses, whether the modern Tropical zodiac common to most Western astrology, or the actual constellations themselves. This latter is the one advocated by Rudolf Steiner and his followers in the Biodynamic movement.[8] But as the Lunarium website rightly says in its article, both traditions 'have a significant number of followers, both have a number of documented experiments supporting their rules', even though the rules are quite different and sometimes 'contradict each other'.

I mention this simply because it's easy to get hung up on various rules and wonder whether or not one is really doing the right thing. This is mostly unnecessary – at any rate, *Gardening and Planting by the Moon* should be viewed as a general guide, not as a set of regulations. Charles Dowding notes in this connection that, 'I think that most of us are mainly governed by fitting our gardening into life's other demands, people and the weather, so there is a danger with prescriptive almanacs that they can make you feel bad for doing a job on the "wrong day". Biodynamics and organics as a whole often feel a little like that to me, as their followers have created a whole code of best practice which can be more daunting than helpful, and you end up feeling guilty for infringing one of the "rules"'[9] Even Rudolf Steiner himself noted that 'Nature is not so cruel as to punish us if we are not paying attention to the phase of the Moon'.

How to Use This Book

Guide to the Calendar

As you can see from the Calendar, there is specific criteria governing the best practices of lunar gardening, including the appropriate times for sowing and planting according to the Moon's phases; which zodiac sign–element the Moon is passing through; the times of Moonrise and Moonset; and then periods when not to plant – namely on an eclipse or a perigee day. The 24-hour clock is used. Then there's the 'barren 'or 'fruitful' signs system (rather less critical to modern lunar gardening) but also the important astrological 'aspects' – the angular distances between the Moon and certain other planets on certain days. This all explained below.

On 3 October 2023, the Calendar shows us that the Moon moved into Gemini, ♊, at 5:04; by the 5th it has moved into the next sign, Cancer, ♋ at 12:33, or 33 minutes past noon. A Flower Day has moved on to a Leaf Day. The Moonrise or Moonset positions (one of the best times to plant or sow) are entered for every day of the year, and on 5 October 2023, the Moon *sets* at 14:56. As it's a Leaf Day, this would be an ideal time to plant any leaf or salad crops. Additionally, on this day, you can also see that the Moon is *trine* to Saturn (exactly 120 degrees away) – ☽ △ ♄ – at 14:54, *also* a good time for Leaf crops. The fact that these two times almost coincide is a happy accident, not always repeated! Occasionally, there are times when aspects happen way too late or early in the day to be appropriate and these are kept to a minimum in the calendar. When this happens, use the time for Moonrise or Moonset, if possible.

My starting point in *Gardening and Planting by the Moon* for appropriate planting or sowing is always the criteria for Plant–Element Days. Then, I factor in any aspects, here between the Moon and the Sun, Moon and Venus or Moon and Saturn. You may choose, of course, to give the Moon's phases supreme importance over the Plant–Element Days. Then, there are periods traditionally *inappropriate* for planting and sowing, namely Perigee days, when the Moon is closest in its orbit to the Earth, and solar or lunar eclipses. Again, both subjects are explained below.

Key to the Symbols

New Moon	Full Moon	First Quarter	Last Quarter
●	○	◑	◐

Moonrise	Moonset	Apogee	Perigee
☽	☾	●	○

Moon	Sun	Venus	Saturn
☽	☉	♀	♄

Conjunction	Sextile	Square	Trine	Opposition
☌	✶	□	△	☍

Solar eclipse	Lunar eclipse
Solar	**Lunar**

Aries	Taurus	Gemini	Cancer	Leo	Virgo
♈	♉	♊	♋	♌	♍
(Fire)	(Earth)	(Air)	(Water)	(Fire)	(Earth)

Libra	Scorpio	Sagittarius	Capricorn	Aquarius	Pisces
♎	♏	♐	♑	♒	♓
(Air)	(Water)	(Fire)	(Earth)	(Air)	(Water)

Plant Days — The Elements

'Before the heavens there existed fire, air, water, earth, which we suppose men to know ... wherefore we are compelled to speak of water or fire, not as substances, but as qualities.'

Plato

Originally, the Four Greek Elements: Fire, Earth Air and Water, were more than mere physical *effects* of nature. Rather, they were considered essential spiritual forces. Plato – the first to use the term 'elements' – boiled them down to their essentials when noting they symbolically stood for *qualities*. That is, a thing's overall characteristics could be expressed both spiritually or physically, metaphorically or concretely. Thus, when astrologers write of the elemental qualities in humans, it's really a shorthand about the behaviour of the original element.

The Fire signs are: Aries ♈; Leo ♌; and Sagittarius ♐
These signs are 'fiery', hot-tempered, inconstant or volatile because this is how actual Fire behaves. Personally, they are animated, lively and project 'warmth', again, like actual Fire.

The Earth signs are: Taurus ♉; Virgo ♍; and Capricorn ♑
These signs rule over the 'reality' function – the everyday world of objects, facts and details that help us make sense of life. An Earthy person is 'solid', 'grounded', dependable, enduring and persevering.

The Air signs are: Gemini ♊; Libra ♎; and Aquarius ♒
Air signs are restless, adaptable, changeable, with a light, casual touch that reaches out and makes social connections – just as actual air crosses boundaries, can't be contained and covers a wide area.

The Water signs are: Cancer ♋; Scorpio ♏; and Pisces ♓
If Air moves around, Water stands still or sinks. These types live for their feelings, always seeking the depths and – like actual water – are reflective and tend to adapt to the shape of their 'environment', in human terms meaning other people.

When the Four Elements were applied to the theory of lunar gardening, it resulted in the categorisation of plants as follows: Fruit-seed Plants (Fire); Root Plants (Earth); Flower Plants (Air) and finally, Leaf Plants (Water). For example, lettuce, celery and bok choy are assigned as 'water plants', and whilst there doesn't seem to be any *obvious* rationale as to why that is, these three make perfect sense as they're all very high in *actual* water content. In fact, they form the top three in the 'vegetables with the highest water content' league table. Lettuce contains 95.6ml of water per 100g, celery comes in at number two with 95.4ml water per 100g, whereas bok choy (or pak choi, a kind of Chinese cabbage) has slightly less water with 95.3ml water per 100g. Justification for these plant–element pairings can also be found in Heinrich Cornelius Agrippa's three-part work on natural philosophy from about 1533: 'In Plants also, the roots resemble the Earth, by reason of their thickness: and the leaves, Water, because of their juice: Flowers, the Aire, because of their subtility, and the Seeds the Fire, by reason of their multiplying spirit.'[10]

Here, Agrippa is attempting to build a bridge between the actual physical properties of a plant, and how it seems to have characteristics of one element or another. Hence, the juice that is present in leaves puts them in the Water category, or how the very fragility, impermanence and even smell of flowers remind one of the ethereal, here-today-gone-tomorrow, nature of Air. The days for Root, Seed, Flower or Leaf show which type of plants are best to work with. As you can see from the calendar, they last for either two or three days, according to which sign–element the Moon happens to be in at any one time. So, let's get down to brass tacks:

FIRE
PLANT DAY: SEED
When the Moon is in a Fire sign, it's the right time to work with (sow, transplant or cultivate):

Apple, Blackberry, Strawberry, Broad bean, Runner bean, French bean, Fig, Plum, Apricot, Cherry, Courgette, Gooseberry, Pumpkin, Asparagus, Peas, Marrow, Nectarine, Aubergine (eggplant), Sweetcorn, Cucumber, Tomatoes, Nuts. Also, according to tradition, if you harvest on a Seed Day, your fruits and seeds should possess better storage quality. For Beekeepers: Seed Days will encourage nectar collection.

EARTH
PLANT DAY: ROOT
When the Moon is in an Earth sign, it's the right time to work with (sow, transplant and cultivate):

Celeriac, Horseradish, Onion, Spring onion, Beetroot (red beet), Ginger, Ginseng, Jerusalem artichoke, Parsnip, Carrot, Leeks, Potato, Swede (Rutabaga), Sweet Potato, Garlic, Mushroom, Radish, Turnip, Turmeric, Parsley. For Beekeepers: encourage your bees to construct more comb.

AIR
PLANT DAY: FLOWER
When the Moon is in an Air sign it's the right time to work with (sow, transplant or cultivate):

Artichokes, Broccoli, Elderflower, Borage, Cauliflower, Flowering plants (of any kind), herbs that are used for medicinal or therapeutic purposes. For Beekeepers: traditonally, brood activity is boosted on a Flower Day, as well as the development of the colony.

WATER
PLANT DAY: LEAF
When the Moon is in a Water sign, it's the right time to work with (sow, transplant or cultivate):

Asparagus, Basil, Bok Choy, Cabbage, Celery, Chicory, Cress, Fennel, Rhubarb, Lettuce, Mint, Mustard, Sage, Sorrel, Spinach, Sprouts, Thyme. Traditionally, harvesting on a Leaf Day is to be discouraged as fruits and vegetables are said to decompose quicker. Also, for Beekeepers, it's a time to rest and avoid activity around the hive.

Lunar Phases for Planting or Harvesting

The main four phases in a lunar month (in what's called the Lunation cycle, the time it takes from one New Moon to the next) are the New Moon, the First Quarter, the Full Moon, and the Second (or Last) Quarter. All have a crucial role to play in lunar gardening; one basic rule of thumb concerns just when to plant according to the Moon's two waxing or waning phases. Plants that grow *above the ground* (like lettuce) should be planted during its waxing time, when the light is increasing. Root plants *beneath the ground* (like potatoes) should be sown or planted when the Moon is waning. It should also be added that the effect of the Moon is not just on the ocean tides, but the groundwater tables which lie below us.

The Moon affects plant growth through a process known as *geotropism* – it's how plants flourish as they react to gravitational pull. We're also considering two opposite directions here: stems and leaves, for example, grow upwards, and roots – of course – move downwards, responding to gravity. All in all, lunar gravitational pull will go through phases of increase and decrease throughout the lunar month. Obviously, a New Moon begins the lunar cycle; there is now a large gravitational pull on the Earth. Also, tides are high. Remember that seeds will assimilate more water at the New Moon when moisture reaches up to the soil surface above. In turn, this will cause the seeds to expand, producing better growth and germination Two or three days before the New Moon is the best time to plant short-and extra-long-germinating seeds (which take about a month to germinate). As we enter the first week of the lunar cycle, plants will enjoy a well-balanced rate of growth between leaves and roots but after about three days the lunar gravitational pull falls away and is *decreased*.

However, during the *second* week of the Lunation, the Moon's gravitational force is actually thrown into reverse – it now gets stronger and *increases*. This has the effect of inhibiting the growth of roots. Light from the Moon (since it's still waxing) is obviously getting stronger – the growth of leaves is stimulated at this time. As Michel Gros, author of *In Tune with the Moon*, points out, plants will increase in vitality with the moonlight, especially as the Full Moon gets nearer.

When we arrive at the Full Moon, its light is now at its most powerful and groundwater at its most plentiful. With peak moisture, roots draw from the water table and this is beneficial for root crops such as potatoes, beets, onions and carrots. Gravitational pull is strong. Harvest fruits and vegetables just before the Full Moon and they'll store very nicely – they'll even boost your vitality when eaten.

As the light begins to diminish slowly as the Moon wanes, by the *third* week of the Lunation cycle, lunar gravitational pull will be decreasing. Leaf growth in plants will slow, yet root growth is stimulated once again as the Moon's gravitational pull diminishes. Remember, more gravitational pull from the Moon and roots slow down their growth; less and they grow faster.

Finally, in the *fourth* and final week of the lunar cycle, moonlight is obviously decreasing while lunar gravitational pull strengthens as we head for the next New Moon. Root growth (and leaf growth) now will slow down.

Lunar Gardening and the Signs of the Zodiac

The notion that the Moon's position in a certain sign will reveal the type of plant most appropriate to work with stems from the intrinsic nature of the four elements. It's a theory adopted by medieval and Renaissance astrology, where zodiac signs are noted as either as *fruitful* or *barren, moist* or *dry,* and *cold* or *hot.* The seventeenth century English astrologer William Lilly, in his *Christian Astrology* wrote, for example, that Cancer, is 'the most fruitful and bountiful Sign, it being the house of the Moon', and so is Pisces, which is 'very fecund and prolificall', and a 'signe of many Children'. Virgo, on the other hand (contradicting the general scheme of things), even 'hath the name of the barren Signe, for Mayds of themselves produce no Births'.

If you favour this scheme in lunar gardening over using the *phases* of the Moon, the outline is as follows:

Fire signs: Aries, Leo, Sagittarius – hot and dry (barren)

Earth signs: Taurus, Virgo, Capricorn – cold, dry (fruitful)

Air signs: Gemini, Libra, Aquarius – hot, moist (barren)

Water signs: Cancer, Scorpio, Pisces – cold, moist (fruitful)

According to this system, sowing and planting should obviously be performed when the Moon is in one of the fruitful signs: Cancer, Scorpio, Pisces, or Taurus, Virgo or Capricorn. Unfortunately, as with many things, astrologers don't always concur. As we can see, for William Lilly, Virgo is a *barren* sign, though I don't see why (according to my many years of astrological knowledge) this should be, so I would argue you may therefore disregard it! Likewise, in Lilly's estimation, both Aquarius and Libra are fruitful, again going against the astrological grain, so to speak.

However, it *does* obviously follow that sowing should be avoided when the Moon is in a barren sign, these days are good, nevertheless, for tasks such as pruning, weeding and deadheading. The rationale ought to be easy to understand – Earth and Water are 'fruitful' as they're the most *fundamental entities* when it comes to the plant world – the sap and soil, if you like. Fire and Air are 'barren' and – though necessary to growth – are *externals,* the Sun and wind. You could think in terms of 'direct' and 'indirect' if you want to dispense with the archaic language. You will also notice my use of the word 'traditional', which implies the opportunity to take things with a pinch of salt. So, traditionally, when the Moon is in:

Aries (barren), a Fire sign: appropriate for preparing the ground with a plough, or for tilling soil. Though 'barren' it may be good for planting garlic, chives or onions. Also, a good sign for pruning.

Taurus (fruitful), an Earth sign: in astrology intimately associated with the natural world – all that is fecund, rural and 'green' is associated with this sign. Good for root crops.

Gemini (barren), an Air sign: best for tidying up flowers, weeding, pest control, using hedge clippers, or cutting grass.

Cancer (fruitful), a Water sign: traditionally associated with nurture, it's extremely fecund and fruitful. Good for any planting or transplanting, watering, irrigation, fertilising.

Leo (barren) a Fire sign: best suited to ploughing or weeding. Cultivation, or pruning of fruit trees can be done, though not traditionally great for planting or transplanting as it's supposedly *extremely* barren.

Virgo (fruitful) an Earth sign: traditionally barren, though as an Earth sign, associated with the harvesting of crops (the symbol is often a Virgin holding an ear of wheat). Good time to plant roots that can be used in home medicines.

Libra (barren), an Air sign: traditionally 'semi-fruitful'. A good time to plant beautiful and/or fragrant flowers or, in fact, perform any type of decorative work that will brighten and prettify your garden.

Scorpio (fruitful), a Water sign: traditionally high in fertility. Scorpio (though a leaf planet) likes to dig deep, so plants that need strong root development are favoured. Otherwise, plant salad crops above ground.

Sagittarius (barren), a Fire sign: like Aries, appropriate for planting onions, garlic, chives. A seed-plant day, good for the care of fruit trees or canes, or ploughing the soil.

Capricorn (fruitful), an Earth sign: traditionally very productive, good for root crops. Also, an appropriate time for the making of garden structures like walls, fences, trellises or garden beds, or to repair them.

Aquarius (barren), an Air sign: according to the contrarian William Lilly, 'without doubt more fruitful than barren'. Useful for weeding and preparing soil and, like Capricorn, the right time to attend garden structures.

Pisces (fruitful), a Water sign: great for root growth and for planting all kinds of crops, especially salad. Also, the appropriate time to work with any kind of aquatic plants or fishponds in your garden.

The Aspects

Aspects are the angular relationships or distances between planetary bodies (or zodiacal degrees like the Ascendant) and when performing a birth chart for a person are indicators of individual psychology, for knowing what makes a person tick. Aspects are usually categorised as either 'hard' or 'soft', and this depends on the degree of zodiacal longitude (around a 360° circle) separating the two bodies. For example, sextiles (60°) and trines (120°) are traditionally 'easy', or 'soft', and conjunctions (0°), squares (90°) and oppositions (180°) are 'difficult' or 'hard'. The implication is that sextiles and trines involve a nice and harmonious flow of energy between the two planets, whilst squares and oppositions entail a kind of conflict, or friction. But in lunar gardening this rule can be interpreted somewhat differently.

The *Gardening and Planting by the Moon* calendar details three traditionally used astrological planets (the Sun, Venus and Saturn) that will come into contact with the Moon at various times of the day. If possible, do your planting close to the times given for the aspects – remembering that the influence of a lunar contact last only about two hours.

Although the planet Saturn has a baneful, restrictive kind of influence (in human affairs) it is central to lunar gardening. Moon–Saturn contacts have especial importance to agriculture and plant development when you consider that Saturn is the only truly 'earth' planet (in the context of the Four Elements) the logic is sound. Saturn, metaphysically, represents how an energy manifests and materialises in the world. Nothing can happen at all without taking on physical form.

Moon–Saturn aspects cover *generally the growth of plant life.* In Roman mythology he was – surprise, surprise – a god who presided over agriculture and the Saturnalia. Also in Numerology, Saturn relates to number four – to *materialisation*, the process of bringing something into being. This also suggests the four seasons or four cardinal points of the compass – abstract ideas that help us find our place and orient ourselves in the world. In the *Gardener's Labyrinth*, from the sixteenth-century, some of the Moon–Saturn contacts are mentioned. With the 60° sextile, '*it is then commended to labour the earth, sow, and plant*', yet for the 90° square it is, '*denied utterly to deal in such matters*'. I have – based on my 30+ years' experience as a professional astrologer – included all of the Moon–Saturn aspects as being valid. Latterday farmers who make use of lunar gardening principles apparently reckon Moon opposition Saturn to be a crucial aspect, yet I see no reason to exclude the square, either.

Moon–Sun aspects are also noted, as one might expect. The Sun is our source of natural light and warmth on Earth and belongs to the Fire element. It infuses things with vitality and energy and is the creative 'multiplying spirit' mentioned by Agrippa. Highly appropriate to Seed Plant days.

Moon–Venus aspects are very useful for Flower Plant days. Venus in astrology is predominantly an 'airy' planet, concerned with surface beauty and whatever is pretty, colourful and pleasing to the eye.

Moonrise and Moonset

The phenomenon of Moonrise is, as the name suggests, when the Moon is becoming visible above the horizon; Moonset, when it is disappearing below it. The exact times of day when Moonrise and Moonset occur depend on where in the lunar phase we are at any one time, but these positions are included as they indicate, in general, the best *times* of day to get busy planting. We naturally want to look at daytime for our gardening, and we have Moonrise when the Moon is *waxing*. When the Moon is *waning* (after the Full Moon) we have Moonset in the daytime instead. The Moonrise and Moonset entries are set for 0 degrees longitude and calculated for London.

Apogee/Perigee and Eclipses — When to Avoid the Garden

Apogee and Perigee are – respectively – the days/times when the Moon is either furthest or nearest to the Earth in her orbit (see *Glossary* pg 94). For Perigee, read this as one of the 'bad' days for planting or sowing. According to Biodynamics pioneer Maria Thun in her book, *Work on the Land and the Constellations*: 'When the Moon recedes from the Earth in the course of its monthly cycle, the effect on plant growth can in some ways be compared with that time of year when the Earth is furthest away from the Sun, ... the tendency in the plant-world is then to run to seed, whereas the growth forces decrease. Thus the effect of the Moon's Apogee on the Seed Plants can still be comparatively beneficial. For the sowing of leaf crops, however, this time is definitely unfavourable. Carrots sown during these days easily become woody. The only plant to react positively to being planted at Apogee is the potato. The Moon's Perigee, which can be compared to midwinter when the Earth is nearer to the Sun, has a very different effect. If we prepare a Seed bed on this day and sow our seeds, germination is poor. Most of these plants are somewhat inhibited in their growth and are also more subject to attacks from fungus diseases and pests. Apogee days are mainly clear and bright, while those at Perigee are mostly dull, heavy or rainy.'[11]

The same pertains to a Lunar or Solar eclipse. Simply put, the solar eclipse is where the shadow of the Moon crosses the Earth's surface; a lunar eclipse is when the Moon is obscured as it moves into the Earth's shadow, on the 'far side' of the Sun. Eclipses can be partial or total, but in the older, traditional astrology they're all portents of doom, indicating disaster of one kind or another. Even modern astrologers are wary of them, as they seem to coincide with drastic change and often unpleasant irreversible events – as if one phase of life has ended completely. Stability is lost temporarily, and one is 'groping in the dark'. It may therefore be good practice to avoid the garden on an eclipse day.

October 2023

October Reminders

Sunday 1

ರ 1:19

☾ 9:39

● New Moon   ◑ First Quarter   ☽ Moonrise
○ Full Moon   ◑ Last Quarter   ☾ Moonset

October 2023

Monday 2

♉

☾ 11:07

Tuesday 3

Harvest fruit crops that can be stored through the winter.

♊ 5:04

☽ △ ☉ 00:03

☾ 12:32

Wednesday 4

♊

☾ 13:50

Thursday 5

An ideal time to sow cabbages in cold frames; better still, try two days before the New Moon.

♋ 12:33

☽ △ ♄ 14:54

☾ 14:56

Friday 6

♋

◑ 13:49

☾ 15:47

Saturday 7

♌ 23:26

☾ 16:24

Sunday 8

♌

☾ 16:50

October 2023

Monday 9

Tomatoes can be grown on this
Seed Day, but only in a hot-bed
or heated greenhouse.

♌

☽ ⚹ ☉ 7:07

☽ 17:08

Tuesday 10

A (Apogee) at 04:41

♍ 12:03

☽ 17:23

Wednesday 11

♍

☽ 17:34

Thursday 12

♍

☽ 17:45

Friday 13

Just before the New Moon, a
great time to plant bulbs such as
crocus, hyacinth, tulip and hardy
alliums.

♎ 00:22

☽ 17:55

Saturday 14

Harvest/Hunter's Moon. Annular
solar eclipse – avoid the garden!

♎

● 17:56

Solar 18:00

☽ 6:53

☽ ☌ ☉ 17:54

No Planting

X

Sunday 15

Plant lettuces in a frame, but
when cold weather sets in cover
with sash and straw matting.
Ready for use in December and
January.

♏ 11:05

☽ 8:07

☽ △ ♄ 12:41

♎	♏	♐	♑	♒	♓
Libra	Scorpio	Sagittarius	Capricorn	Aquarius	Pisces
Air	*Water*	*Fire*	*Earth*	*Air*	*Water*

October 2023

Monday 16

♏

☽ 9:24

Tuesday 17

♐ 19:38

☽ 10:44

Wednesday 18

♐

☽ 12:05

Thursday 19

Peas can be sown in open ground without transplanting, but remember to thin out the plants.

♐

☽ 13:21

☽ ✶ ☉ 19:01

Friday 20

♑ 1:56

☽ 14:26

☽ ✶ ♄ 3:09

Saturday 21

♑

☽ 15:15

Sunday 22

Sow broccoli in a cold frame and leave the plants there over the winter months, ensuring enough warmth.

♒ 6:07

◐ 3:31

☽ 15:50

☽ □ ☉ 3:29

| ♀ Venus | ☉ Sun | △ Trine | ♂ Conjunction |
| ♄ Saturn | □ Square | ✶ Sextile | ☍ Opposition |

October 2023

Monday 23

♒

☽ 16:14

Tuesday 24

Plant spring cabbages outdoors and winter lettuces in frames or under cloches.

♓ 8:34

☽ △ ☉ 9:44

☽ 16:32

Wednesday 25

♓

☽ 16:47

Thursday 26

P (Perigee) at 04:02 No planting on a Perigee day!

♈ 10:03

☽ 17:00

No Planting

✗

Friday 27

♈

☽ 17:13

Saturday 28

Partial lunar eclipse – avoid the garden!

♉ 11:45

○ 20:25

Lunar 20:15

☾ 7:06

☽ ⚹ ♄ 12:39

No Planting

✗

Sunday 29

Daylight Saving Time ends at 02.00.

♉

☽ ☍ ☉ 21:32

☾ 7:34

● New Moon
○ Full Moon
◑ First Quarter
◐ Last Quarter
☽ Moonrise
☾ Moonset

October 2023

Monday 30

♊ 15:09

☾ 9:02

Tuesday 31

Samhain (sow-in): the Celtic
equivalent to Halloween,
signifying the end of the harvest
season.

♊

☾ 10:26

Gardening Notes

♈	♉	♊	♋	♌	♍
Aries	Taurus	Gemini	Cancer	Leo	Virgo
Fire	*Earth*	*Air*	*Water*	*Fire*	*Earth*

November 2023

November Reminders

Wednesday 1

Lettuces can still be sown, though in a cold frame – keep them there over winter with some protection; plant out in spring when the soil is softer.

♋ 21:31

☾ 11:40

☽ △ ♄ 22:28

Thursday 2

♋

☾ 12:39

Friday 3

Why not get the garden tidy? Rake up any fallen leaves into a pile to make a leaf mould.

♋

☾ 13:22

☽ □ ☉ 8:36

Saturday 4

This is possibly the best month for planting new nut trees, as long as the soil is warm enough. This is also the best day!

♌ 7:21

☾ 13:52

Sunday 5

Bonfire Night

♌

◑ 8:38

☾ 14:14

♎	♏	♐	♑	♒	♓
Libra	Scorpio	Sagittarius	Capricorn	Aquarius	Pisces
Air	Water	Fire	Earth	Air	Water

November 2023

Monday 6
A (Apogee) at 21:48

♏ 19:39

☾ 14:30

Tuesday 7

♏

☾ 14:42

Wednesday 8

♏

☾ 14:53

Thursday 9
Finish off planting bulbs and bulbous perennials. Also put any hardy annuals under cloches to prevent weather damage.

♎ 8:08

☾ ♂ ♀ 10:22

☾ 15:03

Friday 10
Ensure that roses are pruned to prevent wind-damage when the Moon is waning.

♎

☾ 15:13

Saturday 11

♏ 18:39

☾ △ ♄ 19:43

☾ 15:24

Sunday 12
Diwali

♏

☾ 15:38

♀ Venus	☉ Sun	△ Trine	♂ Conjunction
♄ Saturn	□ Square	✳ Sextile	♊ Opposition

November 2023

Monday 13

Time to make your hotbeds for winter lettuces; also to trench/store celery for use in the spring.

♏

● 9:29
☽ 7:26

☽ ☌ ☉ 9:27

Tuesday 14

♐ 2:23

☽ 8:48

Wednesday 15

♐

☽ 10:09

Thursday 16

Now, mushrooms can be planted in a dark space such as a cellar, barn or under the benches of your greenhouse.

♑ 7:42

☽ 11:20

☽ ⚹ ♄ 8:48

Friday 17

♑

☽ 12:14

Saturday 18

♒ 11:28

☽ 12:53

Sunday 19

An apt time for planting winter flowers such as heather, hellebores and snowdrops.

♒

☽ 13:20

☽ △ ♀ 8:11

● New Moon   ◑ First Quarter   ☽ Moonrise
○ Full Moon   ◐ Last Quarter   ☾ Moonset

November 2023

Monday 20

A good time to collect any fallen leaves for later use as a compost.

♓ 14:30

◑ 10:51

☽ 13:39

☽ □ ☉ 10:49

Tuesday 21

P (Perigee) at 21:01. No planting on a Perigee day!

♓

☽ 13:54

No Planting

✗

Wednesday 22

An excellent time to plant or transplant fruit trees or bushes such as apples, pears or plums.

♈ 17:20

☽ 14:07

☽ △ ☉ 17:34

Thursday 23

♈

☽ 14:19

Friday 24

Plant your root vegetables this afternoon around 14.30.

♉ 20:29

☽ 14:33

Saturday 25

♉

☽ 14:48

Sunday 26

♉

☽ 15:08

♈	♉	♊	♋	♌	♍
Aries	Taurus	Gemini	Cancer	Leo	Virgo
Fire	Earth	Air	Water	Fire	Earth

November/December 2023

Monday 27

♊ 00:40

○ 9:17
☾ 7:59

Tuesday 28

With the waning Moon, an excellent time to prune any fruit trees.

♊

☾ 9:18

☽ △ ♀ 17:54

Wednesday 29

Though hardly exciting, maintain your garden by continuing to remove fallen leaves.

♋ 6:54

☾ 10:25

☽ △ ♄ 8:50

Thursday 30

St Andrew's Day, patron saint of Scotland.

♋

☾ 11:15

Friday 1

♌ 16:01

☾ 11:51

Saturday 2

Winter is mostly about garden tasks and preparation: when the ground freezes, give strawberry beds a winter-covering of marsh hay, etc.

♌

☾ 12:16

☽ △ ☉ 11:44

Sunday 3

Advent (Christian festival) begins.

♌

☾ 12:35

| ♎ Libra *Air* | ♏ Scorpio *Water* | ♐ Sagittarius *Fire* | ♑ Capricorn *Earth* | ♒ Aquarius *Air* | ♓ Pisces *Water* |

December 2023

Monday 4
A (Apogee) at 18:41

℞ 3:50

☾ 12:48

Tuesday 5
Choose well-ripened onion bulbs for winter storage and keep in a dry, airy place.

℞

◖ 5:50

☾ 13:00

Wednesday 6

♎ 16:35

☾ 13:10

Thursday 7

♎

☾ 13:20

Friday 8

♎

☾ 13:31

Saturday 9
Mustard or cress can be sown (every week, even) in a greenhouse or frame for a good succession.

♏ 3:35

☾ 13:43

☽ △ ♄ 6:33

Sunday 10

♏

☾ 13:59

| ♀ Venus | ☉ Sun | △ Trine | ♂ Conjunction |
| ♄ Saturn | ☐ Square | ✶ Sextile | ☍ Opposition |

December 2023

Monday 11

♐ 11:11

☾ 14:21

Tuesday 12

♐

● 23:33

☽ 7:47

Wednesday 13

Uproot parsnips for winter use and store them in sand, perhaps in the cellar or on a greenhouse shelf.

♑ 15:32

☽ 9:04

Thursday 14

♑

☽ 10:07

Friday 15

♒ 17:56

☽ 10:52

Saturday 16

P (Perigee) at 18:52 No planting on a Perigee day!

♒

☽ □ ♀ 17:32

☽ 11:23

No Planting

X

Sunday 17

This leaf day is a good time to plant out lettuces that were sown earlier in October.

♓ 19:59

☽ ✶ ☉ 12:03

☽ 11:45

● New Moon ◑ First Quarter ☽ Moonrise
○ Full Moon ◐ Last Quarter ☾ Moonset

December 2023

Monday 18

♓

☽ 12:01

Tuesday 19

Just after noon, prune any grape-vines and make the first application of winter sprays for fruit trees.

♈ 22:47

◑ 18:40

☽ 12:15

☽ □ ☉ 18:39

Wednesday 20

♈

☽ 12:27

Thursday 21

♈

☽ 12:40

Friday 22

Winter solstice 03:28; the true onset of winter and the shortest day.

♉ 2:50

☽ 12:54

☽ ✶ ♄ 2:46

Saturday 23

On this Root day, why not plant some mushrooms in a light-restricted place.

♉

☽ 13:11

Sunday 24

Christmas Eve

♊ 8:15

☽ 13:35

♈	♉	♊	♋	♌	♍
Aries	Taurus	Gemini	Cancer	Leo	Virgo
Fire	*Earth*	*Air*	*Water*	*Fire*	*Earth*

December 2023

Monday 25
Season's greetings – it's
Christmas Day!

♊

☽ 14:07

Tuesday 26
Boxing Day

♋ 15:15

☽ △ ♄ 20:29

☽ 14:52

Wednesday 27

♋

○ 00:34

☾ 9:07

Thursday 28

♋

☾ 9:49

Friday 29
Late in the year is nut tree
planting season – hazel, sweet
chestnuts and walnuts can be
planted this morning.

♌ 00:23

☾ 10:18

Saturday 30

♌

☾ 10:38

Sunday 31
New Year's Eve/Hogmanay. Time
to harvest swedes that have been
left in the ground.

♍ 11:54

☾ 10:54

♎	♏	♐	♑	♒	♓
Libra	Scorpio	Sagittarius	Capricorn	Aquarius	Pisces
Air	Water	Fire	Earth	Air	Water

January 2024

Monday 1
New Year's Day. A (Apogee) at 15:28.

♍

☽ △ ☉ 8:58

☾ 11:06

Tuesday 2

♍

☾ 11:17

Wednesday 3
Sow begonias, carnations, petunias and sweet peas indoors.

♎ 00:47

☽ ⚹ ♀ 12:15

☾ 11:26

Thursday 4

♎

◑ 3:32

☾ 11:36

Friday 5

♏ 12:40

☽ △ ♄ 19:48

☾ 11:48

Saturday 6
Epiphany, Twelfth Day after Christmas – seek out a recipe for Twelfth Night Cake.

♏

☾ 12:02

Sunday 7
Plant fruit trees, bushes and any type of cane. Also, currants, grapes and gooseberries may be pruned now.

♐ 21:09

☾ 12:20

| ♀ Venus | ☉ Sun | △ Trine | ☌ Conjunction |
| ♄ Saturn | □ Square | ⚹ Sextile | ☍ Opposition |

January 2024

Monday 8

♐

☾ 12:47

Tuesday 9

♐

☾ 13:27

Wednesday 10

Sow onion seeds in cold frames or boxes under glass.

♑ 1:34

☾ 14:26

☽ ⚹ ♄ 8:28

Thursday 11

♑

● 11:58

☽ 8:44

☽ ☌ ☉ 11:57

Friday 12

♒ 3:02

☽ 9:22

Saturday 13

P (Perigee) at 10:34 No planting on a Perigee day!

♒

☽ 9:48

☽ ⚹ ♀ 7:31

No Planting

✗

Sunday 14

♓ 3:29

☽ 10:06

| ● New Moon | ◑ First Quarter | ☽ Moonrise |
| ○ Full Moon | ◐ Last Quarter | ☾ Moonset |

January 2024

Monday 15
A good time to sow salad crops at Moonrise.

♓

☽ ✳ ☉ 20:46

☽ 10:21

Tuesday 16
A Seed Day appropriate for sowing peas, beans or like crops.

♈ 4:49

☽ 10:34

Wednesday 17

♈

☽ 10:47

Thursday 18
Sow onion seeds and carrots under glass; also radishes can be sown in hotbeds or anywhere that provides shelter and warmth.

♉ 8:12

☽ ✳ ♄ 16:56

◑ 3:54

☽ 11:00

Friday 19

♉

☽ 11:17

Saturday 20
Plant hyacinths indoors, or sow begonias, petunias, sweet peas or carnations.

♊ 13:58

☽ 11:38

Sunday 21

♊

☽ 12:07

♈	♉	♊	♋	♌	♍
Aries	Taurus	Gemini	Cancer	Leo	Virgo
Fire	*Earth*	*Air*	*Water*	*Fire*	*Earth*

January 2024

Monday 22

☊ 21:51

☽ 12:47

Tuesday 23

Sow salad crops like lettuce, radish and cress with the Moon–Saturn trine.

☊

☽ 13:40

☽ △ ♄ 8:14

Wednesday 24

☊

☽ 14:46

Thursday 25

The Wolf Moon is January's Full Moon. Also, the Buddhist (Mahayana version) New Year begins today.

♌ 7:37

○ 17:55

☾ 8:20

Friday 26

A good day to sow early peas and beans, in cold frames or under cloches.

♌

☾ 8:43

Saturday 27

♍ 19:12

☾ 9:00

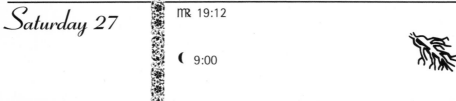

Sunday 28

♍

☾ 9:13

♎	♏	♐	♑	♒	♓
Libra	Scorpio	Sagittarius	Capricorn	Aquarius	Pisces
Air	*Water*	*Fire*	*Earth*	*Air*	*Water*

January 2024

Monday 29

A (Apogee) at 08:14

♍ ℞

☽ 9:24

Tuesday 30

♎ 8:04

☽ 9:33

Wednesday 31

A good time for pruning your climbing roses if you haven't yet done so; also, plant St. Brigid anemones outside if the weather's mild enough.

♎

☽ 9:43

☽ △ ☉ 6:06

Gardening Notes

♀ Venus   ☉ Sun   △ Trine   ♂ Conjunction

♄ Saturn   ☐ Square   ✷ Sextile   ☍ Opposition

February 2024

February Reminders

Thursday 1

Celtic Fire Festival of *Imbolc*, to signify the end of winter. Prepare the ground for early sowing.

♏ 20:38

☾ 9:53

Friday 2

Candlemas (Christian). Plant early cucumbers indoors as the Moon aspects Saturn.

♏

☽ △ ♄ 9:38

◑ 23:19

☾ 10:06

Saturday 3

♏

☾ 10:21

Sunday 4

♐ 6:28

☾ 10:43

● New Moon   ◐ First Quarter   ☽ Moonrise

○ Full Moon   ◑ Last Quarter   ☾ Moonset

February 2024

Monday 5

Sow any summer-flowering plants in the greenhouse when the Moon aspects the Sun.

♐

☽ ✳ ☉ 11:55

☾ 11:15

Tuesday 6

Cover your seed beds with cloches.

♑ 12:10

☾ 12:04

Wednesday 7

♑

☾ 13:12

Thursday 8

♒ 14:01

☾ 14:38

Friday 9

Sow cauliflowers indoors, also hardy annuals outside that will bloom early.

♒

☽ ♂ ☉ 22:58

● 23:00

☽ 7:47

Saturday 10

P (Perigee) at 18:52, No planting on a Perigee day! Chinese New Year, Year of the Dragon.

♓ 13:44

☽ 8:09

No Planting

✗

Sunday 11

♓

☽ 8:25

♈	♉	♊	♋	♌	♍
Aries	Taurus	Gemini	Cancer	Leo	Virgo
Fire	*Earth*	*Air*	*Water*	*Fire*	*Earth*

February 2024

Monday 12

♈ 13:27

☽ 8:39

Tuesday 13

Shrove Tuesday (Christian)

♈

☽ 8:52

Wednesday 14

Potato seeds can be chitted in egg cartons – if you're an early riser, do this with the Moon–Sun sextile!

♉ 15:03

☽✶☉ 6:39

☽ 9:06

Thursday 15

♉

☽ 9:21

Friday 16

Harvest winter bulbs that have now flowered and create indoor displays: Eastern cyclamen, crocus, snowdrops and certain types of daffodil.

♊ 19:41

◐ 15:02

☽ 9:41

Saturday 17

♊

☽ 10:07

Sunday 18

♊

☽ 10:44

| ♎ Libra *Air* | ♏ Scorpio *Water* | ♐ Sagittarius *Fire* | ♑ Capricorn *Earth* | ♒ Aquarius *Air* | ♓ Pisces *Water* |

February 2024

Monday 19
Plant asparagus or lettuces under cloches.

♋ 3:25

☽ △ ♄ 20:02

☽ 11:34

Tuesday 20

♋

☽ 12:36

Wednesday 21
Sow hardy annuals under cloches at this time for early blooms.

♌ 13:41

☽ 13:47

Thursday 22

♌

☽ 15:01

Friday 23

♌

☽ 16:15

Saturday 24
Plant garlic, Jerusalem artichokes or asparagus under cloches.

♍ 1:38

☽ ☍ ☉ 12:30

○ 12:32

☾ 7:21

Sunday 25
A (Apogee) at 14:59.

♍

☾ 7:32

| ♀ Venus | ☉ Sun | △ Trine | ☌ Conjunction |
| ♄ Saturn | ☐ Square | ✶ Sextile | ☍ Opposition |

February 2024

Monday 26
Time to bring in bulbs for indoor flowering as and when they are ready.

♎ 14:30

☾ 7:42

Tuesday 27

♎

☾ 7:51

Wednesday 28

♎

☾ 8:01

Thursday 29
Leap Day (every four years) but beware, folklore tells us that broad beans grow the wrong way in a Leap Year!

♏ 3:09

☾ 8:12

Gardening Notes

March 2024

March Reminders

Friday 1

St David's Day, patron saint of Wales.

♏

☾ 8:26

Saturday 2

♐ 13:56

☾ 8:45

Sunday 3

Plant or transplant outdoors apples, apricot, blackberry, cherry, raspberries or strawberries.

♐

☽ □ ☉ 15:23

◑ 15:25

☾ 9:11

♈ Aries Fire	♉ Taurus Earth	♊ Gemini Air	♋ Cancer Water	♌ Leo Fire	♍ Virgo Earth

March 2024

Monday 4

♑ 21:15

☾ 9:51

Tuesday 5

Sow carrots, parsnips, garlic or radishes when the Moon sextiles Saturn.

♑

☾ ⚹ ♄ 15:37

☾ 10:48

Wednesday 6

♑

☾ 12:04

Thursday 7

♒ 00:40

☾ 13:33

Friday 8

A splendid time for working with flowers – plant some roses or summer-flowering bulbs when the Moon meets lovely Venus.

♒

☾ ☌ ♀ 18:55

☾ 15:08

Saturday 9

Summer cabbages can now be sown (under cloches or in a cold frame for transplanting in May or June.

♓ 1:04

☾ ☌ ♄ 18:22

☾ 16:43

Sunday 10

P (Perigee) at 07:04. No planting! Also, Mothering Sunday and Ramadan begins.

♓

☾ ☌ ☉ 9:00

● 9:02

☽ 6:44

No Planting

♎ Libra *Air*   ♏ Scorpio *Water*   ♐ Sagittarius *Fire*   ♑ Capricorn *Earth*   ♒ Aquarius *Air*   ♓ Pisces *Water*

March 2024

Monday 11

♈ 00:20

☽ 6:57

Tuesday 12

♈

☽ 7:10

Wednesday 13

Plant onions, carrots or swede, and sow parsnips in the early evening with the Moon–Saturn sextile.

♉ 00:29

☽ 7:25

☽ ✶ ♄ 19:29

Thursday 14

♉

☽ 7:43

☽ ✶ ☉ 17:56

Friday 15

♊ 3:17

☽ 8:07

Saturday 16

Sow hardy annual flowers outdoors (although under cloches). Sow carnation seed in boxes and set out the young plants as early as you can.

♊

☽ 8:41

Sunday 17

St Patrick's Day – patron saint of Ireland

♋ 9:42

☽ 4:12

☽ 9:27

♀ Venus	☉ Sun	△ Trine	☌ Conjunction
♄ Saturn	☐ Square	✶ Sextile	☍ Opposition

March 2024

Monday 18
Sow indoors your cucumbers, celery or courgettes.

♋

☽ △ ♄ 8:28

☽ 10:26

Tuesday 19

♌ 19:34

☽ △ ☉ 18:52

☽ 11:35

Wednesday 20
Vernal Equinox 03:08, the start of spring in the Northern Hemisphere.

♌

☽ 12:49

Thursday 21

♌

☽ 14:03

Friday 22

♍ 7:43

☽ 15:16

Saturday 23
A (Apogee) at 15:45

♍

☽ 16:27

Sunday 24
Palm Sunday

♎ 20:39

☽ 17:37

● New Moon   ◐ First Quarter   ☽ Moonrise
○ Full Moon   ◑ Last Quarter   ☾ Moonset

March 2024

Monday 25
Annual lunar eclipse – avoid the garden!

♎

○ 7:01

Lunar 7:14

☾ 6:01

☽ ☌ ☉ 7:00

No Planting

✗

Tuesday 26

♎

☾ 6:10

Wednesday 27

♏ 9:04

☾ 6:21

Thursday 28
Maundy (Holy) Thursday. A good day to sow summer cabbage, spinach and lettuce for later transplanting.

♏

☾ 6:34

☽ △ ♄ 7:00

Friday 29
Good Friday

♐ 19:53

☾ 6:50

Saturday 30
An appropriate time for planting tomatoes, though in heated greenhouses.

♐

☾ 7:13

☽ △ ☉ 15:44

Sunday 31
The clocks move forward 1 hour to Daylight Saving Time. Also, it's Easter Sunday.

♐

☾ 8:47

♈	♉	♊	♋	♌	♍
Aries	Taurus	Gemini	Cancer	Leo	Virgo
Fire	*Earth*	*Air*	*Water*	*Fire*	*Earth*

April 2024

Monday 1

All Fool's Day, the origins of which date from the *Hilaria* of ancient Rome.

♑ 4:06

☾ 9:36

Tuesday 2

Hindu New Year (Nav Varsh) begins.

♑

◑ 3:16

☾ 10:43

Wednesday 3

♒ 9:09

☾ 12:05

Thursday 4

Sow indoors any annual bedding plants; use the time of the Moon–Sun sextile if appropriate.

♒

☽ ⚹ ☉ 10:44

☾ 13:35

Friday 5

♓ 11:14

☾ 15:07

Saturday 6

As it's a Leaf Day, sow herb seeds, such as basil, chives or parsley, under cloches or in cold frames.

♓

☽ ☌ ♄ 10:09

☾ 16:39

Sunday 7

P (Perigee) at 18:50 No planting on a Perigee day!

♈ 11:26

☾ 18:10

No Planting

♎	♏	♐	♑	♒	♓
Libra	Scorpio	Sagittarius	Capricorn	Aquarius	Pisces
Air	*Water*	*Fire*	*Earth*	*Air*	*Water*

April 2024

Monday 8
Total solar eclipse – avoid the garden!

♈

● 18:22

Solar 18:18

☽ 6:15

☽ ☌ ☉ 18:20

No Planting

✗

Tuesday 9
Ramadan ends

♉ 11:24

☽ 6:29

Wednesday 10
Sow beetroot, carrots or turnips outdoors when the Moon contacts Saturn.

♉

☽ 6:45

☽ ✳ ♄ 11:16

Thursday 11

♊ 13:00

☽ 7:06

Friday 12
Plant outside sweet peas and summer-flowering bulbs such as anemones, acidanthera, nerines.

♊

☽ 7:36

Saturday 13
This morning, outside, it's time to sow Brussels sprouts, lettuce and summer spinach.

♋ 17:46

☽ 8:17

☽ ✳ ☉ 6:34

Sunday 14

♋

☽ 9:13

♀ Venus   ☉ Sun   △ Trine   ☌ Conjunction

♄ Saturn   □ Square   ✳ Sextile   ☍ Opposition

April 2024

Monday 15

Winter cabbages can now be sown for transplanting in late June or July.

◔ 19:14

☽ 10:21

☽ □ ☉ 19:12

Tuesday 16

A good time for sowing melon (indoors).

♌ 2:25

☽ 11:35

Wednesday 17

♌

☽ 12:50

Thursday 18

Onion sets and maincrop potatoes should be planted around noon with the Sun–Moon trine.

♍ 14:12

☽ 14:04

☽ △ ☉ 12:01

Friday 19

♍

☽ 15:15

Saturday 20

A (Apogee) at 03:10

♍

☽ 16:25

Sunday 21

Dead-head any tulips or daffodils.

 3:09

☽ 17:35

| ● New Moon | ◑ First Quarter | ☽ Moonrise |
| ○ Full Moon | ◐ Last Quarter | ☾ Moonset |

April 2024

Monday 22
♎

☽ 18:45

Tuesday 23
St George's Day, patron Saint of England, although historians are certain he wasn't actually English!

♏ 15:21

○ 23:50

☾ 5:30

Wednesday 24
St. Mark's Eve, when the Devil oversees the yearly blossoming and seeding of fern, hence this date is also called the Devil's Harvest.

♏

☾ 5:42

☽ △ ♄ 22:51

Thursday 25
♏

☾ 5:57

Friday 26
Not too late for sowing tomato seeds in a seed tray (in a propagator or heated greenhouse).

♐ 1:38

☾ 6:18

Saturday 27
♐

☾ 6:48

Sunday 28
♑ 9:39

☾ 7:33

♈	♉	♊	♋	♌	♍
Aries	Taurus	Gemini	Cancer	Leo	Virgo
Fire	*Earth*	*Air*	*Water*	*Fire*	*Earth*

April 2024

Monday 29

VS

A good time to plant turmeric for use in home remedies – it prefers warm, humid weather and well-drained soil.

☽ ⚹ ♄ 15:28

☾ 8:34

Tuesday 30

♒ 15:21

With this Moon–Venus aspect, a good time to sow half-hardy annuals that will flower in pots later on.

☽ □ ♀ 18:04

☾ 9:50

Gardening Notes

♎	♏	♐	VS	♒	♓
Libra	Scorpio	Sagittarius	Capricorn	Aquarius	Pisces
Air	*Water*	*Fire*	*Earth*	*Air*	*Water*

May 2024

May Reminders

Wednesday 1

Beltane (May Day) one of the four Gaelic seasonal festivals marking the start of summer. Sow biennials outdoors today.

♒

◗ 11:28

☾ 11:16

Thursday 2

⚹ 18:53

☾ 12:45

Friday 3

Sow (outdoors) Brussels sprouts and lettuces when the Moon sextiles the Sun.

♓

☾ 14:13

☽ ⚹ ☉ 17:54

Saturday 4

♈ 20:42

☾ 15:41

Sunday 5

P (Perigee) at 23:04 No planting on a Perigee day!

♈

☾ 17:09

No Planting

X

♀ Venus   ☉ Sun   △ Trine   ♂ Conjunction

♄ Saturn   □ Square   ⚹ Sextile   ☍ Opposition

May 2024

Monday 6
Bank Holiday

♉ 21:43

☾ 18:39

Tuesday 7

♉

☾ 20:11

Wednesday 8
Plant or transplant hardy annuals in the open.

♊ 23:22

● 3:23
☽ 5:07

Thursday 9
Lavender, a 'medicinal flower' good for anxiety, stress, and blood pressure, can now be planted as the soil gets warmer.

♊

☽ 5:32

Friday 10

♊

☽ 6:08

Saturday 11

♋ 3:14

☽ 6:58

Sunday 12
Sow salad crops such as chicory, cress, lettuce, in the open with this helpful sextile.

♋

☽ ✶ ☉

☽ 8:03

● New Moon   ◐ First Quarter   ☽ Moonrise
○ Full Moon   ◑ Last Quarter   ☾ Moonset

May 2024

Monday 13

♌ 10:37

☽ 9:17

Tuesday 14

♌

☽ 10:33

Wednesday 15

At the time of the Sun–Moon square, sow root vegetables like swedes, carrots, turnips, parsnips.

♍ 21:34

◑ 11:49

☽ 11:49

☽ □ ☉ 11:47

Thursday 16

♍

☽ 13:01

Friday 17

A (Apogee) at 19:58

♍

☽ 14:12

Saturday 18

♎ 10:23

☽ 15:21

Sunday 19

Pentecost/Whit Sunday (Christian)

♎

☽ 16:31

♈	♉	♊	♋	♌	♍
Aries	Taurus	Gemini	Cancer	Leo	Virgo
Fire	*Earth*	*Air*	*Water*	*Fire*	*Earth*

May 2024

Monday 20
♏ 22:34

☽ 17:43

Tuesday 21
♏

☽ 18:58

Wednesday 22
When the Moon trines Saturn this morning, plant or transplant Brussels sprouts, cabbages, celeriac, chicory.

♏

☽ △ ♄ 10:02

☽ 20:16

Thursday 23
The 'Flower Moon' associated with growth and fertility – prune fruit trees and canes. Also, Buddhist Vesak Day.

♐ 8:25

☽ ☍ ☉ 13:52

○ 13:54

☾ 4:22

Friday 24
♐

☾ 4:50

Saturday 25
♑ 15:37

☾ 5:30

Sunday 26
Trinity Sunday (Christian)

♑

☾ 6:26

| ♎ Libra Air | ♏ Scorpio Water | ♐ Sagittarius Fire | ♑ Capricorn Earth | ♒ Aquarius Air | ♓ Pisces Water |

May 2024

Monday 27
Spring Bank Holiday

♒ 20:46

☾ 7:40

Tuesday 28
Plant begonias, carnations or chrysanthemums indoors when the Moon trines the Sun.

♒

☾ 9:04

☽ △ ☉ 9:53

Wednesday 29

♒

☾ 10:31

Thursday 30
Sow savoy cabbage with the Sun–Moon square - the result will be small hearts for winter use.

♓ 00:34

◑ 17:14

☾ 11:58

☽ □ ☉ 17:12

Friday 31

♓

☾ 13:24

Gardening Notes

♀ Venus   ☉ Sun   △ Trine   ☌ Conjunction
♄ Saturn   □ Square   ✳ Sextile   ☍ Opposition

June 2024

June Reminders

Saturday 1

Capsicums may be planted out today, in a warm sheltered area.

♈ 3:29

☾ 14:50

Sunday 2

P (Perigee) at 08:16. No planting on a Perigee day!

♈

☾ 16:16

No Planting

● New Moon   ◐ First Quarter   ☽ Moonrise

○ Full Moon   ◑ Last Quarter   ☾ Moonset

June 2024

Monday 3

♉ 5:56

☾ 17:44

Tuesday 4

Sow onions that can be used for salad.

♉

☾ 19:14

☽ ⚹ ♄ 13:45

Wednesday 5

♊ 8:37

☾ 20:42

Thursday 6

Chamomile, a 'medicinal flower' good for anxiety, stress, insomnia, can be sown in May, and planted (or planted out) this month – in a sunny place with free-draining soil.

♊

● 12:39

☽ 4:02

☽ ☌ ♀ 13:35

Friday 7

An appropriate time for sowing lettuce (outdoors) and planting cucumbers (inside).

♋ 12:42

☽ 4:45

Saturday 8

♋

☽ 5:44

Sunday 9

♌ 19:30

☽ 6:56

♈	♉	♊	♋	♌	♍
Aries	Taurus	Gemini	Cancer	Leo	Virgo
Fire	*Earth*	*Air*	*Water*	*Fire*	*Earth*

June 2024

Monday 10
Begin your summer pruning today of red and white currants and gooseberries.

♌

☽ 8:13

Tuesday 11

♌

☽ 9:30

Wednesday 12

♍ 5:40

☽ 10:45

Thursday 13
Mushrooms may be prepared for growing with the Moon–Saturn opposition. Get some horse-manure as a fertiliser, if possible.

♍

☽ ☍ ♄ 20:17

☽ 11:56

Friday 14
A (Apogee) at 14:35

♎ 18:13

◑ 5:20

☽ 13:06

Saturday 15
Evening primrose/moonflower, a 'medicinal flower' good for mild skin conditions and inflammation, can be planted now in well-drained/light moist soil.

♎

☽ 14:16

Sunday 16
Sow any hardy annuals (outside), such as calendials, cornflowers or chrysanthemums.

♎

☽ 15:26

♎	♏	♐	♑	♒	♓
Libra	Scorpio	Sagittarius	Capricorn	Aquarius	Pisces
Air	*Water*	*Fire*	*Earth*	*Air*	*Water*

June 2024

Monday 17

♏ 6:39

☽ 16:39

Tuesday 18

♏

Around 18.00 is a good time for planting aquatic plants like water lilies; ensure you have the correct depth of water.

☽ △ ♄ 20:18

☽ 17:56

Wednesday 19

♐ 16:33

☽ 19:15

Thursday 20

♐

Summer solstice 20:52; the true onset of summer and the longest day.

☽ 20:33

Friday 21

♑ 23:10

☽ 21:44

Saturday 22

♑

This month's Full Moon is a 'Strawberry Moon', named after the short season for harvesting strawberries in North America.

○ 1:09

☾ 4:15

Sunday 23

♑

☽ ✶ ♄ 9:01

☾ 5:24

June 2024

Monday 24

♒ 3:15

☾ 6:47

Tuesday 25

Sow biennials such as foxglove for flowering in 2025.

♒

☾ 8:16

Wednesday 26

♓ 6:09

☾ 9:45

☽ △ ☉ 15:25

Thursday 27

P (Perigee) at 12:30. No planting on a Perigee day!

♓

☾ 11:12

☽ ☌ ♄ 14:56

No Planting

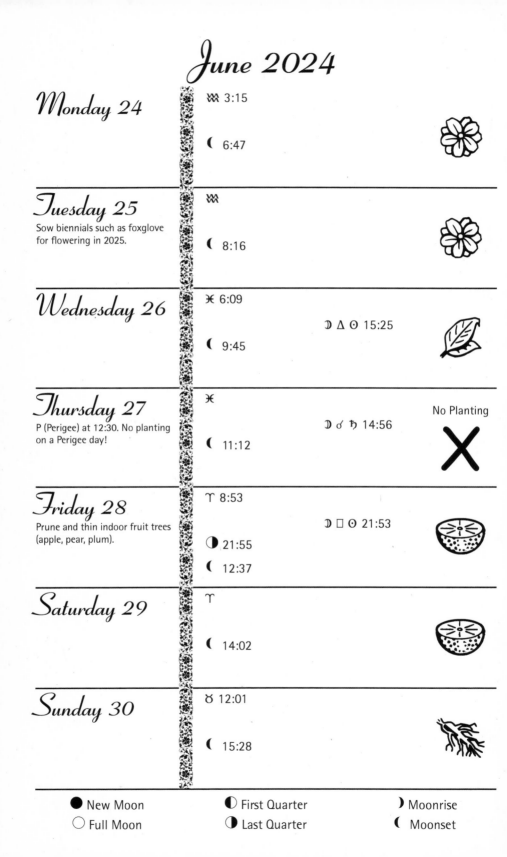

Friday 28

Prune and thin indoor fruit trees (apple, pear, plum).

♈ 8:53

◑ 21:55

☾ 12:37

☽ □ ☉ 21:53

Saturday 29

♈

☾ 14:02

Sunday 30

♉ 12:01

☾ 15:28

● New Moon   ◑ First Quarter   ☽ Moonrise
○ Full Moon   ◐ Last Quarter   ☾ Moonset

July 2024

Monday 1

Sow beetroot and carrots outdoors, late in the day at the time of the sextle (if convenient).

♉

☽ 16:55

☽ ⚹ ♄ 21:27

Tuesday 2

♊ 15:51

☽ 18:22

Wednesday 3

Outdoors, a time to sow forget-me-nots, pansies or hollyhocks.

♊

☽ 19:44

Thursday 4

Celery can be planted out if we have showery weather. Too late to sow now!

♋ 20:53

☽ 20:54

☽ □ ♄ 1:57

Friday 5

♋

● 22:58

☽ 3:30

Saturday 6

A good day to work with leaf vegetables with this Moon–Saturn trine.

♋

☽ 4:37

☽ △ ♄ 8:09

Sunday 7

Pinch out shoots from tomatoes and melons. Islamic New Year (Hijra) begins.

♌ 3:57

☽ 5:53

♈	♉	♊	♋	♌	♍
Aries	Taurus	Gemini	Cancer	Leo	Virgo
Fire	*Earth*	*Air*	*Water*	*Fire*	*Earth*

July 2024

Monday 8

♌

☽ 7:11

Tuesday 9

Summer-sown root plants like beet, onion, carrot, radish and turnip are on the agenda this afternoon.

♍ 13:49

☽ 8:27

Wednesday 10

♍

☽ 9:40

Thursday 11

♍

☽ 10:51

Friday 12

A (Apogee) at 09:11

♎ 2:08

☽ ✶ ♀ 3:14

☽ 12:01

Saturday 13

Encourage flowers to bloom today by deadheading; also trim off any faded foliage.

♎

◑ 22:50

☽ 13:10

Sunday 14

♏ 14:53

☽ 14:22

♎	♏	♐	♑	♒	♓
Libra	Scorpio	Sagittarius	Capricorn	Aquarius	Pisces
Air	Water	Fire	Earth	Air	Water

July 2024

Monday 15

St Swithun's Day: according to weather lore if it's fine today it will be so for forty more days, but if it rains ... you've guessed it!

♏

☽ 15:36

Tuesday 16

Sow any quick-growing varieties of salads when the Sun–Moon trine occurs.

♏

☽ 16:53

☽ △ ☉ 15:04

Wednesday 17

♐ 1:26

☽ 18:12

Thursday 18

♐

☽ 19:26

Friday 19

♑ 8:15

☽ 20:29

Saturday 20

Sow any fast-growing variety of root vegetable when the sextile occurs.

♑

☽ 21:15

☽ ✶ ♄ 17:15

Sunday 21

The July Full Moon is traditionally called the Buck Moon, a reference to male deer growing new antlers this month.

♒ 11:44

○ 10:18

☾ 4:22

| ♀ Venus | ☉ Sun | △ Trine | ☌ Conjunction |
| ♄ Saturn | □ Square | ✶ Sextile | ☍ Opposition |

July 2024

Monday 22

♒

☾ 5:52

Tuesday 23

Shortly after the Full Moon, mow the lawn. Remember to do this once a fortnight to maintain its health in dry periods.

♓ 13:24

☾ 7:24

Wednesday 24

P (Perigee) at 06:41. No planting on a Perigee day!

♓

☾ 8:55

☽ ☌ ♄ 20:31

No Planting

Thursday 25

Morning or evening are the apt times for pruning fruit trees and bushes – gooseberries, raspberry canes – and thinning out apricots or peaches.

♈ 14:53

☾ 10:23

☽ △ ☉ 20:28

Friday 26

♈

☾ 11:49

Saturday 27

♉ 17:24

☾ 13:16

Sunday 28

♉

◑ 2:53

☾ 14:43

● New Moon   ◑ First Quarter   ☽ Moonrise
○ Full Moon   ◐ Last Quarter   ☾ Moonset

July 2024

Monday 29

Ⅱ 21:29

☾ 16:10

Tuesday 30

Good time to dead-head roses and summer bedding plants as the Moon is waning.

Ⅱ

☾ 17:33

☽ ✶ ☉ 11:15

Wednesday 31

Time to plant autumn bulbs like colchicums or nerines.

Ⅱ

☾ 18:46

☽ ✶ ♀ 17:32

Gardening Notes

♈	♉	Ⅱ	♋	♌	♍
Aries	Taurus	Gemini	Cancer	Leo	Virgo
Fire	*Earth*	*Air*	*Water*	*Fire*	*Earth*

August 2024

August Reminders

Thursday 1

Lughnasa (or the Christian Lammas), the third of four Celtic seasonal festivals (held on 1 August) and marking the start of the harvest season.

♋ 3:20

☾ 19:43

Friday 2

With this Moon–Saturn trine, sow cucumber indoors that will fruit in November.

♋

☽ △ ♄ 13:31

☾ 20:24

Saturday 3

Prune sideshoots on apple trees and gooseberry bushes in single cordons.

♌ 11:11

☾ 20:53

Sunday 4

♌

☽ ☌ ☉ 11:12

● 11:14

☽ 4:54

| ♎ Libra *Air* | ♏ Scorpio *Water* | ♐ Sagittarius *Fire* | ♑ Capricorn *Earth* | ♒ Aquarius *Air* | ♓ Pisces *Water* |

August 2024

Monday 5
Bank Holiday (Scotland)

♍︎ 21:18

☽ 6:11

Tuesday 6
Sow some turnips or swedes at this morning's Moonrise.

♍︎

☽ 7:25

Wednesday 7

♍︎

☽ 8:37

☽ ☍ ♄ 9:43

Thursday 8

♎︎ 9:33

☽ 9:47

Friday 9
A (Apogee) at 02:31. Sow hardy annuals and biennials inside: antirrhinums, sweet Williams and pansies.

♎︎

☽ 10:56

☽ ✳ ☉ 21:44

Saturday 10

♏︎ 22:35

☽ 12:07

Sunday 11
Traditionally, today is Old Lammas Eve, a time for folk magic when farmers cut down rowan trees.

♏︎

☽ 13:19

| ♀ Venus | ☉ Sun | △ Trine | ♂ Conjunction |
| ♄ Saturn | □ Square | ✳ Sextile | ☍ Opposition |

August 2024

Monday 12
Spring cabbages can now be sown, for transplanting in September or October.

♏

☽ △ ♄ 10:28

◑ 15:20

☽ 14:34

Tuesday 13
♐ 10:02

☽ 15:51

Wednesday 14
♐

☽ □ ♄ 19:38

☽ 17:07

Thursday 15
Sow Japanese variety onions outside.

♑ 17:52

☽ 18:14

Friday 16
♑

☽ 19:07

Saturday 17
♒ 21:46

☽ 19:46

Sunday 18
♒

☽ 20:13

● New Moon   ◑ First Quarter   ☽ Moonrise
○ Full Moon   ◑ Last Quarter   ☾ Moonset

August 2024

Monday 19
The August Full Moon is known as the Green Corn Moon because the corn is now ripe and ready for harvest.

♓ 22:53

☽ ☍ ☉ 18:25

○ 18:27

☾ 4:52

Tuesday 20

♓

☾ 6:25

Wednesday 21
P (Perigee) at 06:02. No planting on a Perigee day!

♈ 23:02

☾ 7:57

No Planting

✗

Thursday 22

♈

☾ 9:27

Friday 23
Harvest tomatoes (if applicable, and if they are ripe) with this waning Moon.

♈

☾ 10:57

Saturday 24

♉ 00:01

☾ 12:26

Sunday 25

♉

☾ 13:56

♈	♉	♊	♋	♌	♍
Aries	Taurus	Gemini	Cancer	Leo	Virgo
Fire	*Earth*	*Air*	*Water*	*Fire*	*Earth*

August/September 2024

Monday 26
Bank Holiday. Cauliflower seeds sown now will produce finer heads next spring and early summer.

♊ 3:05

☽ □ ☉ 9:25

◐ 9:27

☾ 15:22

Tuesday 27
With the Moon waning, prune any summer flowering shrubs and plants such as lavender and wisteria.

♊

☽ □ ♄ 9:01

☾ 16:39

Wednesday 28

♋ 8:49

☾ 17:42

Thursday 29
Harvest time for summer lettuces if they've been well watered in hot weather.

♋

☽ △ ♄ 15:57

☾ 18:27

Friday 30

♌ 17:10

☾ 18:58

Saturday 31

♌

☾ 19:20

Sunday 1

♌

☾ 19:35

♎ Libra *Air*

♏ Scorpio *Water*

♐ Sagittarius *Fire*

♑ Capricorn *Earth*

♒ Aquarius *Air*

♓ Pisces *Water*

September 2024

Monday 2

♍︎ 3:50

☾ 19:48

Tuesday 3

Prepare for the months to come by sowing winter vegetables.

♍︎

● 1:57

☽ 6:25

☾ ☍ ♄ 12:37

Wednesday 4

♎︎ 16:13

☽ 7:35

Thursday 5

A (Apogee) at 15:53. Summer cauliflowers can be sown indoors for planting out next spring.

♎︎

☽ 8:45

☾ ☌ ♀ 9:12

Friday 6

♎︎

☽ 9:54

Saturday 7

♏︎ 5:20

☽ 11:06

Sunday 8

With the Moon-Sun sextile, a good time to sow winter lettuces under cloches or in the greenhouse.

♏︎

☽ 12:19

☾ ✳ ☉ 13:37

| ♀ Venus | ☉ Sun | △ Trine | ☌ Conjunction |
| ♄ Saturn | □ Square | ✳ Sextile | ☍ Opposition |

September 2024

Monday 9

♐ 17:27

☽ 13:35

Tuesday 10

♐

☽ 14:50

Wednesday 11

Plant or transplant strawberries; also tomatoes can be picked if ripe. Seeds sown now in greenhouses will produce plants fruiting in March.

♐

◑ 6:07

☽ 16:00

☽ □ ☉ 6:05

Thursday 12

♑ 2:39

☽ 16:58

Friday 13

Sow turnips and radishes this evening; also potatoes that are ready can be taken up - with some care!

♑

☽ 17:42

☽ △ ♄ 6:52

Saturday 14

♒ 7:55

☽ 18:13

Sunday 15

Collect seeds and sow (indoors) hardy annuals that will flower in pots in the greenhouse.

♒

☽ 18:35

☽ △ ♀ 19:08

● New Moon   ◑ First Quarter   ☽ Moonrise
○ Full Moon   ◐ Last Quarter   ☾ Moonset

September 2024

Monday 16

♓ 9:40

☽ 18:52

Tuesday 17

♓

☽ 19:06

Wednesday 18

P (Perigee) at 14:23 and a partial lunar eclipse. No planting! The Full Moon is the Harvest Moon.

♈ 9:25

○ 2:36

Lunar 2:45

☾ 6:53

Thursday 19

♈

☾ 8:25

Friday 20

♉ 9:04

☾ 9:58

Saturday 21

Onions, depending on when sown, can be successfully harvested and hung outside if it's warm and dry

♉

☾ 11:32

☽ ⚹ ♄ 9:27

Sunday 22

Autumnal Equinox 12:45, the start of autumn in the Northern hemisphere.

♊ 10:24

☾ 13:03

☽ △ ☉ 10:13

♈	♉	♊	♋	♌	♍
Aries	Taurus	Gemini	Cancer	Leo	Virgo
Fire	*Earth*	*Air*	*Water*	*Fire*	*Earth*

September 2024

Monday 23

♊

(14:27

Tuesday 24

September is for planting out cabbages or lettuces, and parsley can be potted or lifted and placed in frames to use in winter.

♋ 14:51

☽ □ ☉ 18:49

◗ 18:51

(15:37

Wednesday 25

♋

☽ △ ♄ 17:51

(16:28

Thursday 26

♌ 22:48

(17:03

Friday 27

Purchase raspberry canes and plant them at the time of the Moon–Sun sextile.

♌

☽ ⚹ ☉ 7:50

(17:27

Saturday 28

According to traditional folklore, the last day of the year you can pick brambles (blackberries). Try it on this Seed Day, therefore!

♌

(17:44

Sunday 29

Michaelmas, traditionally speaking, the end of harvesting, indeed, the farming year itself.

♍ 9:43

(17:57

♎	♏	♐	♑	♒	♓
Libra	Scorpio	Sagittarius	Capricorn	Aquarius	Pisces
Air	*Water*	*Fire*	*Earth*	*Air*	*Water*

September 2024

Monday 30

 ♏

In a sheltered area you can sow onions successfully with this Moon–Saturn aspect.

☾ 18:07

☽ ☍ ♄ 14:37

Gardening Notes ————————————————

♀ Venus ☉ Sun △ Trine ♂ Conjunction
♄ Saturn ☐ Square ✴ Sextile ☍ Opposition

October 2024

Tuesday 1	♎ 22:21 ☾ 18:17		🌸
Wednesday 2 A (Apogee) at 20:39. Annular solar eclipse – avoid the garden! Rosh Hashanah, Jewish New Year, begins at sundown (and ends at nightfall on the 4th).	♎ ● 18:50 Solar 18:46 ☽ 6:34	☽ ☌ ☉ 18:49	No Planting **X**
Thursday 3	♎ ☽ 7:44		🌸
Friday 4	♏ 11:23 ☽ 8:55		🍃
Saturday 5 Plant out larger types of cabbage but allow two feet between the plants. Also, sow or plant lettuces in a warm greenhouse.	♏ ☽ 10:08	☽ △ ♄ 15:45	🍃
Sunday 6	♐ 23:35 ☽ 11:23		🍊

● New Moon ◐ First Quarter ☽ Moonrise
○ Full Moon ◑ Last Quarter ☾ Moonset

October 2024

Monday 7

♐

☽ 12:38

Tuesday 8

A highly appropriate time to plant or transplant peaches, nectarines or figs in a greenhouse.

♐

☽ 13:49

☽ ⚹ ☉ 5:48

Wednesday 9

♑ 9:39

☽ 14:51

Thursday 10

♑

☽ ⚹ ♄ 11:16

◐ 18:56

☽ 15:38

Friday 11

♒ 16:32

☽ 16:13

Saturday 12

♒

☽ 16:37

Sunday 13

Earth up celery if the weather is fine and dry.

♓ 19:56

☽ □ ♀ 11:07

☽ 16:55

♈	♉	♊	♋	♌	♍
Aries	Taurus	Gemini	Cancer	Leo	Virgo
Fire	Earth	Air	Water	Fire	Earth

October 2024

Monday 14

♓

☽ 17:10

Tuesday 15

♈ 20:35

☽ 17:23

Wednesday 16

♈

☽ 17:36

Thursday 17

P (Perigee) at 01:51. No planting on a Perigee day! The Hunter's Moon is the name for October's Full Moon which, according to folklore, assists hunters in search of prey.

♉ 20:01

○ 11:28

☾ 7:20

☽ ☍ ☉ 11:26

No Planting

✗

Friday 18

♉

☾ 8:55

☽ ⚹ ♄ 17:12

Saturday 19

♊ 20:08

☾ 10:30

Sunday 20

With the waning Moon, cut back any rambler roses or deciduous climbing plants that are outdoors.

♊

☾ 12:02

☽ ☍ ♀ 00:29

♎	♏	♐	♑	♒	♓
Libra	Scorpio	Sagittarius	Capricorn	Aquarius	Pisces
Air	*Water*	*Fire*	*Earth*	*Air*	*Water*

October 2024

Monday 21

♋ 22:51

☽ 13:21

Tuesday 22

Winter spinach sown with this trine will make a good plant before winter.

♋

☽ 14:22

☽ △ ♄ 22:16

Wednesday 23

♋

☽ 15:03

Thursday 24

♌ 5:25

☽ 8:04

☽ 15:32

☽ □ ☉ 8:02

An apt time to sow broad beans on dry warm soils or for a first crop.

Friday 25

♌

☽ 15:51

Saturday 26

♍ 15:49

☽ 16:05

Sunday 27

Clocks revert to Greenwich Mean Time at 02:00.

♍

☽ 15:16

☽ ☍ ♄ 17:55

♀ Venus   ☉ Sun   △ Trine   ☌ Conjunction

♄ Saturn   □ Square   ✷ Sextile   ☍ Opposition

October 2024

Monday 28

St Simon and St Jude's Day and – according to tradition – the onset of wet and windy days, marking the real end of summer.

♍

☾ 15:26

Tuesday 29

A (Apogee) at 22:50

♎ 4:31

☾ 15:35

Wednesday 30

Cauliflowers can be sown again in a frame or in the greenhouse.

♎

☽ ✶ ♀ 11:38

☾ 15:45

Thursday 31

Gaelic seasonal festival of Samhain (sow-in) or All Hallows Eve, denoting the end of the harvest season.

♏ 17:30

☾ 15:55

Gardening Notes

November 2024

November Reminders

Friday 1

Diwali. Plant lettuces in cold frames on this New Moon/Leaf Day.

♏

● 12:48

☽ 6:56

☽ ☌ ☉ 12:46

Saturday 2

♏

☽ 8:11

Sunday 3

Though what can be sown outdoors lessens this month, broad beans and peas are still contenders.

♐ 5:21

☽ 9:27

♈	♉	♊	♋	♌	♍
Aries	Taurus	Gemini	Cancer	Leo	Virgo
Fire	*Earth*	*Air*	*Water*	*Fire*	*Earth*

November 2024

Monday 4
♐
☽ 10:40

Tuesday 5
♑ 15:18
☽ 11:45

Wednesday 6
Jerusalem artichokes can now be harvested – some can even be preserved in sand for use during frosts.
♑
☽ 12:36
☽ ⚹ ♄ 15:16

Thursday 7
♒ 22:59
☽ 13:14

Friday 8
Now is the optimum time for planting your tulip bulbs in pots and borders.
♒
☽ 13:41

Saturday 9
♒
☽ 5:57
☽ 14:00

Sunday 10
Remembrance Sunday
♓ 4:01
☽ 14:15
☽ ⚹ ♀ 00:23

♎	♏	♐	♑	♒	♓
Libra	Scorpio	Sagittarius	Capricorn	Aquarius	Pisces
Air	*Water*	*Fire*	*Earth*	*Air*	*Water*

November 2024

Monday 11
Sea kale may be lifted for forcing in a warm, dark place, but ensure it has strong roots to start with.

♓

☽ 14:29

☽ △ ☉ 13:16

Tuesday 12
♈ 6:27

☽ 14:41

Wednesday 13
♈

☽ 14:54

Thursday 14
P (Perigee) at 11:14. No planting on a Perigee day!

♉ 7:00

☽ 15:10

No Planting

✗

Friday 15
The Beaver Moon is November's Full Moon, so called due to the practice of setting beaver traps by the natives of North America.

♉

○ 21:30

☾ 6:50

☽ ☍ ☉ 21:28

Saturday 16
♊ 7:10

☾ 8:25

Sunday 17
♊

☾ 9:53

♀ Venus   ☉ Sun   △ Trine   ☌ Conjunction
♄ Saturn   □ Square   ✶ Sextile   ☍ Opposition

November 2024

Monday 18

♋ 8:51

☾ 11:05

Tuesday 19

Around noon is a good time to put some rough manure on any rhubarb beds.

♋

☾ △ ♄ 6:47

☾ 11:57

Wednesday 20

As we're in a 'barren' sign, begin to prepare for next year's crops by trenching, manuring and collecting waste to burn in a 'smother'.

♌ 13:52

☾ △ ☉ 11:19

☾ 12:31

Thursday 21

Don't forget to order any seeds in advance well before stocks run dry.

♌

☾ 12:55

Friday 22

♍ 23:02

☾ 13:11

Saturday 23

Carrots can be sown in cold frames, and successive sowings made every three or four weeks until next February.

♍

◑ 1:29

☾ 13:24

Sunday 24

Prune climbing plants, indoors or out.

♍

☾ 13:34

● New Moon ◐ First Quarter ☽ Moonrise
○ Full Moon ◑ Last Quarter ☾ Moonset

November 2024

Monday 25

♎ 11:21

☽ ⚹ ☉ 19:31

☽ 13:44

Tuesday 26

A (Apogee) at 11:55

♎

☽ 13:53

Wednesday 27

Plant or transplant roses, deciduous trees and shrubs, and hardy perennials.

♎

☽ □ ♀ 00:06

☽ 14:03

Thursday 28

♏ 00:22

☽ 14:15

Friday 29

At around 14:30, sow watercress in damp soil or on the outer edges of hotbeds.

♏

☽ △ ♄ 18:50

☽ 14:31

Saturday 30

St Andrew's Day, one of Jesus's disciples and patron saint of Scotland.

♐ 11:54

☽ 14:53

♈	♉	♊	♋	♌	♍
Aries	Taurus	Gemini	Cancer	Leo	Virgo
Fire	*Earth*	*Air*	*Water*	*Fire*	*Earth*

December 2024

December Reminders

Sunday 1

Advent (Christian). Raspberry and blackberry canes and gooseberry and blueberry bushes can be planted now provided weather and soil are suitable.

♐

☽ ☌ ☉ 6:21

● 6:23

☽ 8:28

♎	♏	♐	♑	♒	♓
Libra	Scorpio	Sagittarius	Capricorn	Aquarius	Pisces
Air	Water	Fire	Earth	Air	Water

December 2024

Monday 2

♑ 21:10

☽ 9:36

Tuesday 3

Clear beds and add some compost, plus get digging over any empty borders and pile on some manure.

♑

☽ ⚹ ♄ 21:16

☽ 10:33

Wednesday 4

♑

☽ 11:15

Thursday 5

♒ 4:22

☽ 11:44

Friday 6

Lily of the Valley crowns can be potted up and forced.

♒

☽ ⚹ ☉ 6:38

☽ 12:06

Saturday 7

♓ 9:50

☽ 12:22

Sunday 8

Put rough manure on any asparagus crops.

♓

☽ □ ☉ 15:26

◐ 15:28

☽ 12:35

| ♀ Venus | ☉ Sun | △ Trine | ♂ Conjunction |
| ♄ Saturn | □ Square | ⚹ Sextile | ☍ Opposition |

December 2024

Monday 9

♈ 13:39

☽ 12:47

Tuesday 10

An apt time to prune any open-grown apples or pears.

♈

☽ 13:00

☽ △ ☉ 22:13

Wednesday 11

♉ 15:56

☽ 13:14

Thursday 12

P (Perigee) at 13:20. No planting on a Perigee day!

♉

☽ 13:31

☽ ✶ ♄ 13:55

No Planting

✗

Friday 13

♊ 17:23

☽ 13:55

Saturday 14

Plant out cauliflowers in the greenhouse.

♊

☽ 14:30

☽ △ ♀ 6:39

Sunday 15

The Cold Moon or Long Night's Moon is December's Full Moon, merely due to the cold, short days experienced at this time of year.

♋ 19:22

○ 9:03

☾ 8:42

☽ ☍ ☉ 9:01

● New Moon   ◗ First Quarter   ☽ Moonrise

○ Full Moon   ◖ Last Quarter   ☾ Moonset

December 2024

Monday 16
Harvest time for winter lettuces that have been grown in a heated greenhouse.

♋

☽ △ ♄ 18:33

☾ 9:44

Tuesday 17
♌ 23:40

☾ 10:26

Wednesday 18
♌

☾ 10:55

Thursday 19
♌

☾ 11:15

Friday 20
Time for harvesting winter vegetables like brassicas, leeks or parsnips.

♍ 7:37

☾ 11:29

Saturday 21
Winter solstice at 09:22, the true onset of winter and the shortest day.

♍

☽ ☍ ♄ 10:38

☾ 11:40

Sunday 22
♎ 19:09

◑ 22:19

☾ 11:50

♈	♉	♊	♋	♌	♍
Aries	Taurus	Gemini	Cancer	Leo	Virgo
Fire	*Earth*	*Air*	*Water*	*Fire*	*Earth*

December 2024

Monday 23

♎︎

☾ 12:00

Tuesday 24

A (Apogee) 07:24. Christmas Eve.

♎︎

☾ 12:10

☽ △ ♀ 10:43

Wednesday 25

Christmas Day – Season's Greetings!

♏︎ 8:07

☾ 12:21

Thursday 26

Boxing Day

♏︎

☾ 12:35

☽ △ ♄ 12:30

Friday 27

♐︎ 19:48

☾ 12:54

Saturday 28

Seed Days are always excellent for working with fruits; December is the month for planting fruit trees or bushes.

♐︎

☾ 13:21

☽ ☐ ♄ 23:14

Sunday 29

♐︎

☾ 14:00

♎︎	♏︎	♐︎	♑︎	♒︎	♓︎
Libra	Scorpio	Sagittarius	Capricorn	Aquarius	Pisces
Air	Water	Fire	Earth	Air	Water

December 2024

Monday 30
Vs 4:38

● 22:28

☽ 14:56

Tuesday 31
New Year's Eve. If you feel like being busy, underground onions can now be planted in rows, set a foot apart.

Vs

☽ ✶ ♄ 7:02

☽ 16:07

Gardening Notes

A Brief Glossary

Air Signs – Gemini, Libra and Aquarius, in this book treated as 'barren'.

Annual – a plant that finishes its life cycle (germination, growth, reproduction and death) in the same season.

Apogee/Perigee – an 'apsis' is the furthest or nearest point in a planet's orbit (or satellite) and its primary body. The apsides of the Moon are called the apogee and perigee: the points furthest from and closest to the Earth during the Moon's orbit.

Aspects – angular distances between two planetary bodies in the zodiac. The planetary aspects used in this book are those between the Moon and a) the Sun; b) Venus; and c) Saturn. The aspects used in *Gardening and Planting by the Moon* are the Conjunction; the Sextile; the Square; the Trine; and the Opposition. *See* individual entries.

Biennial – a plant that finishes its life cycle in two years with germination and growth in the first twelve months; reproduction and death in the next.

Chitting – placing seed potatoes in a tray or egg box in a bright, cool but frost-free place to encourage sprouting.

Cloche – a glass or plastic structure that is placed over plants to protect them against frost. The word is French for 'bell', which traditional cloches resemble.

Cold frame – low, glass, insulated frame (somewhat like a tiny greenhouse) that create a suitable environment for young plants that need to adjust to outdoor temperatures.

Conjunction – an aspect separating planets or mathematical points on a birth chart by 0–6°. In astrology, its effects depend on the nature of the planets involved, and whether they combine easily.

Dead-head – to remove spent blooms (heads) on a flower to stimulate further growth.

Deciduous – a plant or tree shedding its leaves every year, usually in autumn/winter.

Direct sow – sowing seeds outdoors exactly where one intends them to crop or flower.

Earth signs – Taurus, Virgo and Capricorn, in this book treated as 'fruitful'.

Earth up – the practice of drawing up soil around a plant base or stem to keep it stable, or guard against frost, or stimulate root growth. Often used in potato cultivation.

Eclipse – a solar eclipse is when the shadow of the Moon crosses the Earth's surface; a lunar eclipse is when the shadow of the Earth crosses the surface of the Moon. Both lunar and solar eclipses are used in this book, and always signify days on which to avoid lunar gardening. Eclipses can be partial or total; with a Lunar Eclipse, a third category is the Appulse, when the Moon enters only the Earth's penumbra. There are several types of Solar Eclipse – two of the most common are the Annular (when the Moon is too distant from the Earth for the apex of its shadow to reach us) and the Annular–Total (which is total for part of its path, but annular for the remainder).

Elements – the four Greek elements used as metaphor in astrology: Fire, Earth, Air and Water. Like the four Jungian psychological types, they are the archetypal 'building blocks' of human psychology. Of fundamental use in lunar gardening, they also correlate with different 'plant type' days, hence Seed Days (Fire); Root Days (Earth); Flower Days (Air) and Leaf Days (Water). Thus, if a certain plant is categorised as a Leaf (say, lettuce), when the Moon is in a Water sign (Cancer, Scorpio or Pisces) one should sow, plant or transplant that plant for optimum results.

Fire signs – Aries, Leo and Sagittarius, in this book treated as 'barren'.

Forcing – obstructing natural light to stimulate and speed up plant growth. This may result in sweeter-tasting stems. Often used with rhubarb and sea kale.

Half-hardy – a plant, whether annual, biennial, perennial or tree/shrub that needs protection outdoors in winter from freezing temperatures (below 0° Celsius/32° Fahrenheit).

Harden off – when young plants growing in protective surroundings are acclimatised to cooler temperatures outside, usually by placing plants outside in daytime and bringing them inside at night.

Hardy – a plant, whether annual, biennial, perennial or tree/shrub that can resist temperatures in winter as low as minus 15° Celsius/5° Fahrenheit.

Hotbed – areas of the garden, often piled up, beneath which exists a layer of fresh animal dung. A composting process occurs when organic compounds decay in the manure. This process in turn produces heat, which helps any plants above.

Lunar phases – *see* waxing and waning Moon

Moonrise and Moonset – these are specific times of the day when the Moon's so-called 'upper limb' can be seen above the horizon (Moonrise) or when it vanishes below it (Moonset). However, the exact times of Moonrise and Moonset are determined by the phase of the Moon at any one time, and its declination, which is its position north or south of the celestial equator, and this is relative to any observer's location. Also, the Moon seems larger at Moonrise or Moonset due to its position close to the horizon.

Opposition – an aspect separating planets or mathematical points on a birth chart by 180°. In astrology it has a challenging effect due to the differences it raises between oneself and others, but it can also lead to greater awareness.

Perennial – a plant whose life cycle lasts more than two years.

Pinching out – the process of removing the growing points on a young plant to stimulate the growth of side-shoots, the minor shoots emanating from the side of the stem.

Plant days – *see* Elements

Planting out – to transplant any seedlings grown indoors to the outdoor areas.

Pot up/pot on – to re-pot seedlings or shoots into a larger pot before transplanting.
Prick out – transferring the seedlings into small individual containers prior to 'potting on' *see* Pot up/Pot on.

Second cropping/second early potatoes – potatoes planted in late summer or early autumn, harvested just over three months (14 weeks) after they were planted.
Seed potatoes – tubers which are grown specially to produce new potato plants.
Seedling – a young, tiny plant that has been grown from a seed.
Sextile – an aspect separating planets or mathematical points on a birth chart by 60°. In astrology it has a mildly beneficial quality.
Square – an aspect separating planets or mathematical points on a birth chart by 90°. In astrology it has a challenging effect that can cause tension and friction, leading the individual to take some kind of action.

Thin/thin out – the process of removing seedlings, shoots, buds or flowers to boost and enhance the growth of those which are left.
Transplanting – the simple process of re-potting young plants into larger pots or into open soil.
Trine – an aspect separating planets or mathematical points on a birth chart by 120°. In astrology it has a beneficial quality, promoting ease and harmony.
Tuber – a tuber, such as a potato, is a tumescent root or sub-surface stem that contains storage tissue.

Water signs – Cancer, Scorpio and Pisces, in this book treated as 'fruitful'.
Waxing and waning Moon – a lunar month, or Lunation, is the length of time it takes from one New Moon to the next. The average time span between two New Moons is approximately 29.5 days or, specifically, 29 days, 12 hours, 44 minutes and 3 seconds. As the Sun and Moon align on the same side of the Earth, and as the Moon 'waxes' in light, the lunar phases progress through New Moon, Crescent Moon, First-quarter Moon, Gibbous Moon, and Full Moon. Afterwards, the Moon 'wanes' in light as it passes through the Gibbous Moon, Third-quarter Moon, Crescent Moon, and back to New Moon.

Notes

1. *The Natural History Of Pliny* (Vol. IV), translated: John Bostock/H. T. Riley, London: Mdccclvi.
2. *The Complete Herbal*, Nicholas Culpeper.
3. https://charlesdowding.co.uk/moon-sowing/
4. https://www.livescience.com/1696-full-moon-sends-dogs-cats-emergency-room.html
5. https://www.newscientist.com/article/dn28051-moons-gravity-could-govern-plant-movement-like-the-tides/
6. https://permacultureprinciples.com/post/moonlight-affect-plant-growth/
7. Recorded in *Mysteries and Symbols in Plants and Gardens*, ed. Paola Maresca, Angelo Pontecorboli pub., Florence, 2012.
8. The Tropical zodiac – aligned to the *seasons* – is the one used in this book and is the same as the 'American' system.
9. *op cit*. Dowding.
10. Heinrich Cornelius Agrippa, *Three Books of Occult Philosophy*
11. https://www.lunarium.co.uk/articles/apogee-perigee/